ELT Playbook
Teacher Training

Sandy Millin

ISBN-13: 978-1-9160698-0-0

Edited by Penny Hands
Any mistakes in the final version of this text are entirely my own, not Penny's!

Credits
Cover design and logo by Ola Walczykowska
Icons taken from The Noun Project (thenounproject.com)
Looking at watch by Gan Khoon Lay
Task completed by Creative Stall
Child question by Christopher Smith
Blog icon by dilayorganci
Mike by Vladimir Belochkin
Blogger by Made
Writing by Martyn Jasinski

With thanks to Natalia Ladygina for helping me to come up with the contents page, to Angelos Bollas, Richard Chinn, Manana Khvichia, Arthur Laing and Matthew Noble for extending the list of further reading, and to Emma Johnston and Gui Henriques for feedback on the tasks and extra ideas.

About the author

Sandy Millin is the Director of Studies at International House Bydgoszcz, Poland. She has worked as an English teacher, manager and CELTA trainer all over the world. She blogs regularly at sandymillin.wordpress.com and tweets @sandymillin. Sandy's first ebook, *Richer Speaking*, was published by the round, and she has subsequently self-published ebooks and print-on-demand paperbacks in the *ELT Playbook* series. Find out more about the whole series at ELTplaybook.wordpress.com.

Table of Contents

Introduction

ELT Playbook Teacher Training aims to fill a hole that I feel exists within English Language Teaching (ELT): guided reflection for those involved in teacher training. This book is based on my work as a CELTA trainer and as somebody who works with teachers taking their first steps in teacher training.

ELT Playbook Teacher Training contains a selection of 30 tasks to help trainers to reflect on what they do, centred on the areas that seem to cause most problems for those new to this aspect of our profession. It can also be used by more experienced trainers, though not all of the tasks may be relevant to everyone.

Why *ELT Playbook*?

According to the Macmillan Dictionary online (accessed 17th August 2017), a playbook is 'any set of strategies to achieve a goal.' I believe it is just such a set of techniques and strategies that teachers and trainers need to develop both inside and outside the classroom to describe themselves as truly professional. This is reflected in the fact that the term 'playbook' has moved from the sportsfield to the boardroom over the last few years.

It is also important to emphasise the 'play' part of 'playbook'. We already have plenty of work to do, so it's important that any professional development we do complements our work in an enjoyable and stimulating way, rather than adding unnecessary extra stress.

Who is this series for?

- Those who want to develop as a teacher or trainer, but who would like some support to learn how to do this, along with clear tasks to work through.
- Teacher trainers or managers who would like ideas for professional development programmes (though please do mention that the ideas are from this book).

And this book?

- Teachers taking their first steps into training, including on courses like the CELTA, as workshops in their schools or as seminars at conferences.
- Those who have not yet started training others and would like a starting point.
- More experienced trainers who would like to consider aspects of their training in a different way.
- Those who would like to develop in a systematic way but are on a limited budget or working in an environment without available support.

Series aims

- To provide a series of tasks you can work through to improve your training.
- To help you to build a professional portfolio that can be used to show your development when applying for jobs.
- To provide guidance in how to reflect on your training.

How does it work?

ELT Playbook Teacher Training is divided into 6 categories, each containing 5 tasks, giving a total of 30 tasks altogether.

The categories are:

1. What is training?
Think about the similarities and differences between teaching and training, and begin to examine your beliefs about what a trainer is and does.

2. Planning training
Look at different elements that make up training and how to fit them together in an effective way for trainees.

3. Observation: written feedback
Critically examine the feedback you and other trainers write to give to trainees. Tip: If you don't have any written feedback to analyse, make notes on a video lesson. Videos can be found at 'Lessons you can watch online' on my blog. See Appendix 3: Further reading on page 71 for the link.

4. Observation: spoken feedback
Consider how you organise spoken feedback sessions and the responses of trainees to what you say.

5. Workshops and input sessions
Analyse the way that you run training sessions.

6. Other aspects
Reflect on areas which fit into other categories, such as varying your training and dealing with challenges.

You can do the tasks in any order: you could start with something you feel you particularly need to work on, you could complete a whole category, or you might prefer to work through the book from beginning to end. If you do one task a week, you should have enough for an average academic year, with a couple of weeks left over to help you when you are particularly busy at work or home. You can also repeat tasks as many times as you like, perhaps reflecting on them in different ways, or seeing how your responses change over time or with different trainees.

Each task has four sections to guide you:

Time

This should give you a rough idea how long the task and reflection will take. You can do them both at the same time, or do the task at one point, and the reflection at another. None of the tasks should take you longer than 2 hours, and many of them should be achievable in under an hour. They are designed to fit in relatively easily around a busy career and the demands of home life. I would be happy for feedback if you feel the timing of any tasks is unrealistic, so this can be edited in future editions of the book.

Task

The basis for your later reflection.

Questions to think about

A series of questions designed to encourage you to think about the task in more depth, considering cause and effect, and the rationale behind key parts of the task. You can answer as many or as few questions as you choose, and there is no obligation to write anything if you don't want to.

Reflection ideas

There are four different possible ways to round off the task, helping you to either share what you find out with the wider teaching community or build up your own private records of your professional development. These could be...

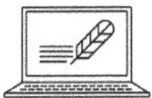

...writing a blog post;

...making a video or audio recording;

...using social media to post an image and some notes;

...or keeping notes in a journal.

These reflection ideas are suggestions, and you are welcome to mix and match them as you see fit.

Learning together

A key objective of the *ELT Playbook* series is to give those who use it the chance to become part of a wider community. The *ELT Playbook* blog at ELTplaybook.wordpress.com is designed to help you find your way around the series. You can also find other members of the community on the following social media channels:

- Facebook: www.facebook.com/ELTplaybook/
- Twitter: www.twitter.com/hashtag/ELTplaybook
- Instagram: www.instagram.com/explore/tags/ELTplaybook/

Via these forums, you will be able to benefit from looking at and commenting on the reflections of other people, and sharing your own reflections if you want to. I hope that these will become large, supportive communities, which we can all enjoy participating in and learning from.

Glossary

I have used some words in particular ways within *ELT Playbook Teacher Training*. These uses may not reflect the way in which they are used in other ELT literature:

- **activity:** anything you would do with students in lessons
- **example lesson:** any complete lesson which is not taught by somebody being trained on the course and which you show to trainees. It could be on video or taught by a trainer
- **session:** any single instance of training, whether that's an in-house workshop, an input session on a training course, a seminar at a conference, or anything else which you believe could be described in this way
- **task:** a task within this book
- **trainee:** anyone who you are working with to improve their teaching. This could include conference sessions or in-school workshops, for example, not just formal courses like CELTA.

What is training? 1: Teaching v. training

Task: 10 minutes
Reflection: 20 minutes

Time yourself for 10 minutes. List anything which is or might be:

- the same when you are teaching and training (e.g. clear instructions are important, I believe students and trainees need a written record of what we've studied in the lesson/session)
- different when you are teaching and training (e.g. I'll be training people I have to work with every day and already know; it's hard to provide practice of what I'm training people to do)

Some of the resources in <u>Appendix 3: Further Reading</u> on page 71 could help you with this.

- Was one category easier or more difficult for you to add to? If yes, why do you think that was the case?
- Are there any items on the list which make the transition from teaching to training smoother or more challenging? For example, being familiar with classroom management techniques can make it easier, but having peers as trainees could be more challenging. Can you think of examples from your own transition?
- Are there any which you hadn't thought about before? Why do you think that is the case?
- How do you think the items on this list might impact on the training you do?
- Are there any areas which you feel you still need to develop in or find out more about? How could you do this?
- Which of the areas are you particularly good at or knowledgeable about? How have you got to this stage? How could you share this knowledge?
- Considering both lists, how would you define training? Do you see it as similar to teaching or different? Why?

Choose one of the areas you identified as a strength and write about the stages you have gone through in your career to reach this level of competence in it.

Describe an example of an idea from your list which made the transition from teaching to training smoother or more challenging for you and why this was the case.

Share a photo of your list using the #ELTplaybook hashtag. Comment on the process of coming up with it and whether it encouraged you to think differently about any aspects of teaching or training.

Choose one of the areas you would like to develop in. Create an action plan with a minimum of three points to show how you will do this. Set a reminder to come back and check whether you've done this later, for example on your phone or using an email alert service.

What is training? 2: The apprenticeship of observation

Task: 10 minutes

Reflection: 20 minutes

Think back to a time when you have been a trainee, for example on a course, in a workshop or at a conference seminar. Write about your memories of the experience. If possible, discuss the experience with somebody else who was also there.

- Is it possible to categorise your memories? What categories would you put them in?
- Did you have any particularly positive or negative memories of the experience? What do you think contributed to this?
- Did the training have any particular impact on your career? Why (not)? Do you think you conduct training in the same way you were trained?
- Did the trainer(s) do or say anything you could 'steal' for your own training? How could you incorporate these things?
- Did they do or say anything you would definitely avoid? What effect did this have on the experience for you?
- If you were able to discuss the experience, did your memories match up with the other person? Why do you think this was?

Choose one of the things you want to 'steal' from this experience. Describe how you could adapt it to your training context.

Talk about the categories you divided your memories into and why you chose them.

Draw a picture or series of pictures to summarise your experience as a trainee in this situation. Share them using the #ELTplaybook hashtag.

Write about your memories of the training experience, indicating which were positive and which were negative and why.

The concept of the 'apprenticeship of observation' was proposed by Dan Lortie, in Schoolteacher: A sociological study (1975, University of Chicago Press) to describe the fact that when you first become a teacher, you have spent many hours as a student observing teachers in action, unlike in other professions like doctors or lawyers. Lortie also suggests that this means that initial training courses can have a weak effect on teachers, in that they will tend to teach as they were taught. I first came across the concept in an IATEFL 2015 presentation by Karla Leal Castañeda, 'The development of cognitions and beliefs on CELTA courses'.

What is training? 3: The wider community

Task: 10 minutes
Reflection: 20 minutes

Draw a mind map of all of the people you have in your professional network who might be able to help you develop as a trainer in the future or who have already done so.

- Which people in your network have you been trained by? Which have you observed doing training? What do you think you have learnt from them?
- Who has most influenced your training so far? In what ways?
- How did you meet the people you have on your mind map?
- How often do you speak to them? When? Is it normally a general conversation or because you have something specific you would like to discuss? How often is it (not) connected to training?
- What kind of questions would you feel able to ask different people on your mind map?
- Are there any questions you might have which you couldn't take to somebody on this mind map? Why?
- How could you find people to add to your network? Where could you meet them? Consider both online and offline places, e.g. a local conference or a facebook group you know about.

Write about three ways in which you have built up your network.

List your ideas for ways to develop your network further.

Share a picture of one of the people who has most influenced your ability to train and note what you have learnt from them and why you chose them. Don't forget to get their permission if necessary. Use the #ELTplaybook hashtag.

Detail some of the questions you feel you could and couldn't ask people on your mind map. Include reasons. Note how you could try to find people or resources to answer those questions.

What is training? 4: Examining your context

Task: 30 minutes
Reflection: 20 minutes

Write a short description of a context you expect to train in soon. Consider the following aspects:

- why the training was requested and by who
- who you will train (background, education, qualifications, English level, etc.)
- what the training will involve
- where you will train (type of institution, facilities available, etc.)
- who you will be working with (co-trainers, managers, etc.)

- Were any of the questions challenging or impossible to answer? Can you think of ways to get the answers?
- Is this a context you have trained in before? If yes, what did you learn the last time that could help you this time? If no, do you know anybody else who has trained in a similar context who could offer you advice?
- Do you think the trainees will find your training useful and/or applicable? Why (not)? If not, how could you adapt it to them? How can you help them to see connections between your training and their everyday work?
- What challenges or opportunities does this context present? How can you counter or exploit them?
- How can you evaluate whether the training you provide is appropriate to the context, while also meeting the needs of the people who requested it?

Describe one of the challenges that this context might present. Suggest two ways you might overcome it. Use the #ELTplaybook hashtag to share what you have written.

Talk about how you plan to exploit at least two of the opportunities this context will provide.

Sketch the place that you will be doing the training, indicating how you can use the space.

Write about how you plan to run the training to make it as useful as possible to the trainees and why you have made those decisions. Include how you plan to evaluate the training.

What is training? 5: Practising what you preach

Task: 10 minutes
Reflection: 20 minutes

Choose a training session you have recently conducted. Alternatively, you could choose one of your recent lessons if you teach as well as doing training. Make a mind map of some of the teaching decisions that you made in the lesson/session. Examples of the type of decisions you made might include how you chose to set up an activity, or how you gave feedback.

- Was the lesson generally reflective of the advice you give when training, or was it very different?
- Imagine you were your own teacher trainer. What feedback would you give yourself on the decisions you made? Are there any decisions you would suggest repeating or avoiding in the future?
- For those you would repeat, how do/could you advise trainees to incorporate something similar in their lessons? Are they already included in the training sessions you run? Would you add them?
- For those decisions you would avoid, why do you think you made them? Are trainees likely to make similar decisions? How can you help them to avoid them?
- How important do you think it is for your teaching to reflect your own training advice? Why?

Choose one of the decisions you made which you would repeat. Describe how to help trainees achieve the same thing in their own classrooms.

Talk through two areas from the feedback you would give yourself on your lesson.

Share your mind map using the #ELTplaybook hashtag. Note whether your lesson/session reflects your advice when training.

Write about whether you think it's important for your own teaching to reflect your training advice and why (not).

Planning training 1: Needs analysis

Task: 10 minutes
Reflection: 15 minutes

List the things you need to know about your trainees before the course. For each, add how you could find this information out, e.g. an interview, an observation, speaking to their manager.

- How much of this information do you already know? What do you still need to find out?
- Which of these methods of needs analysis do you think would be particularly useful or practical? Why?
- Are there any methods which might not be very practical? Why? In what situations might you still be able to use them?
- Which of these methods have you tried in the past? How successful were they? Would you change anything about how you set up that kind of analysis if you used it again?
- For the needs analysis methods which you would like to try, what would be the ideal situation to use them in? Will you have an opportunity to try them out in any of your upcoming training?
- How could you collate the results of your needs analyses? How can you apply them to the training you will be doing?

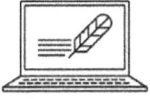

Describe one of the methods of needs analysis you have tried in the past, how successful it was, and what you would change if you used it again.

Discuss how you could collate the results of your needs analyses, and how you can apply them to the training you will be doing.

Share a photo of your list using the #ELTplaybook hashtag. Say which types of analyses you will conduct for your next session/course, and how you will run them.

Make a needs analysis action plan for your next session/course, stating which information you still need to find out about your trainees and how you will go about doing this.

Planning training 2: Linking content and practice

Task and reflection: 30 minutes altogether

Look back at a training session you have done and answer the following questions.

- Did you explicitly ask trainees to reflect on teaching they had done before the session in relation to the topic of your training at any point?
- Did they reflect on how their teaching might change after the session as a result of the training?
- If yes, at what point in the session did this happen? Do you think it benefitted the trainees? How? If not, was this a conscious decision? Why?
- Were there any points where you could have added these links? How? Would they refer to practice before the session or after? Why?
- Were there any points where you had links between content and practice but they didn't work the way you wanted them to? In future, would you change or remove them? If you changed them, how would you do this? If you removed them, what else could you do in the session instead?
- What kind of trainees do you think might need explicit links between training content and teaching practice to be made by the trainer in the session? Who could do this with less or no trainer help?
- How many different ways can you think of to link content to practice, either supported by the trainer during a session or independently by trainees afterwards? Two ideas to start you off are choosing an activity which didn't work and coming up with three ways to change it in future, or thinking of which class you could use a new activity with.

Describe how you linked content and practice within the session and why. Alternatively, say why you didn't include these links.

Talk about your thoughts regarding the links between content and practice in training, and what kind of support different trainees might need to make these links.

Draw two or three pictures representing different ways to link content and practice in a training session. Share them using the #ELTplaybook hashtag.

Write about whether you would change the links between content and practice if you ran the session again, as well as why and how, if applicable.

Planning training 3: Tracking development

Task: 10 minutes, plus 3 x 15 minutes
Reflection: 20 minutes

Choose one trainee you are working with at the moment. Write a list of 3-5 questions you can ask them to track their development over time based on one part of the training you have done. For example: 'Which activities from the session have you tried out with your students?' or 'Which idea from the session do you keep thinking about?'

Speak to them for 15 minutes three times during the time you spend with them to discuss this part of the training. If you only do one-off training, find out if somebody in one of your sessions is willing to speak to you a few times after the session. You might choose to change your questions as you repeat this process.

- What questions did you ask? Why did you choose these questions?
- Did you use the same questions each time? If yes, did the trainee give similar answers each time? If no, what did you choose to change and why?
- Did the trainee give the kind of answers you expected? Did they volunteer any extra information? Did anything they say make you want to change your training in the future? Or did it confirm that the training you did is useful as it stands?
- Over time, did the trainee's response to your training change? What do you think influenced those changes?
- Do you think that discussions like this are a useful way to track the development of trainees based on training you have given them? Why (not)? Is it something you would do again?
- What other methods could you use to track trainee development based on training you have done?

Share your list of questions using the #ELTplaybook hashtag. Say why you chose these questions and whether you changed any of them.

With your trainee's permission, record one of the fifteen-minute discussions. At the end, add one or two minutes saying what you learnt about your training from the discussion.

Draw a flowchart showing your impressions of the development of your trainee from before the training session through to after your final discussion with them. Don't forget to get their permission if you want to share it.

Write about what you learnt about your training from the process of discussing it with one of your trainees, as well as whether this might influence you to change anything in your future training.

Planning training 4: Evaluating training

Task: 45 minutes
Reflection: 30 minutes

Create a questionnaire you can use to evaluate the success of some teacher training you have been involved in, either as a trainer or a participant. Aspects you could consider include:

- relevance of content
- mode of delivery
- participant engagement
- timing and pacing
- use of resources

Complete it yourself. If possible, ask other trainers/trainees to complete it too.

- What process did you go through to create your questionnaire?
- How did you decide on the questions you included in the questionnaire?
- Having completed it, would you change any of the questions?
- Did the responses to the questionnaire reveal anything interesting or surprising about the training?
- If you were a participant on the course, what feedback would you give to the trainer based on the results?
- If you were a trainer, what would you now change if you ran the training again? What should stay the same?
- If other people completed the questionnaire, did their answers match up to yours?
- What did you learn from the process of creating this questionnaire and reflecting on the answers to it? Would you do something like this again? Why (not)?

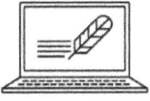

Write about the process of creating the questionnaire and how you decided on what questions to include. Say whether you would do something similar again.

Describe what you learnt from the process of completing the questionnaire and reflecting on the results.

Show us your questionnaire using the #ELTplaybook hashtag. Comment on any questions you would now change.

Summarise the feedback for the trainer based on the results of the questionnaire, and what should be changed or maintained if the training is repeated.

Planning training 5: Desert island resources

Task: up to 20 minutes (depending on how long it takes you to decide!)
Reflection: 30 minutes

Imagine that you are going to conduct a training course on a desert island, and you can only take a limited set of resources with you. Choose eight books or blogs that would be useful for the kind of trainees you typically teach, plus one video. Alternatively, choose eight videos and one book or blog.

- How would you describe the trainees you made your desert island resource list for?
- What were your criteria for selecting the material you included on the list?
- What process did you go through to make the list?
- How easy or difficult was it for you to meet the requirement of 8 + 1? Did you need to search for more resources to get to nine items or cut your list down from more?
- Have you read the book(s) or blog(s) you recommended? Have you watched the video(s)? How long ago? How often?
- What did you get out of these resources yourself? What do you think your trainees will get out of them?
- Will you pass the list on to your trainees? Why (not)? If yes, what form would it be most useful to present the list in?
- If the waves came in and you had to choose just one of the resources you selected to save for your desert island training course, which would it be? Why?

Share your list using the #ELTplaybook hashtag, along with a general description of the trainees you made it for.

Talk about the criteria you used to select your list.

Take a photo or screenshot of the one book or video you would save from the waves on your desert island, and say why. Don't forget to ask for permission if necessary.

Write about the process of making your list, and what you have learnt about yourself as a trainer as a result.

This task was inspired by the long-running BBC Radio 4 series Desert Island Discs.

Observation: Written feedback 1: What is 'good'?

Task: 10 minutes; 30 minutes if you don't already have written feedback to analyse, watch two videos for about 15 minutes each – see <u>Appendix 3: Further Reading</u> on page 71 for sources of videos.

Reflection: 20 minutes

Look back at two pieces of written feedback you have given to trainees: one for a lesson that went well, and one for a weaker lesson. Highlight the words 'good' or 'great' each time they appear. Circle any other phrasing you have used, positive or negative, which stands out to you.

- How similar is your written feedback style for the stronger and weaker lessons? Why do you think this is? Is there anything you would like to change about either of them?
- What phrases are 'good' and 'great' used in? Do they stand alone or are they modifying a noun, e.g. 'good instructions'? How useful do you think they are? Can you think of alternative phrasing you could have used at any point?
- If you don't use 'good' and 'great' much, what phrasing do you tend to use instead for positive comments?
- What other phrasing stood out to you? Why? Were they positive or negative comments?
- When looking at negative comments, how do you think your phrasing might come across to the trainee? On reflection, would you change any of the wording? Why (not)?
- What did you learn about the kind of language you use in your written feedback as a result of this analysis?

List useful phrases for written feedback, either which you already use or which you would like to incorporate in future. Share your list using the #ELTplaybook hashtag.

Say what you have learnt about the language you use in your written feedback from this process.

With the trainee's permission, share a snapshot of some of your written feedback. Comment on your choice of phrasing and how useful you think it is to a trainee.

List similarities and differences between your written feedback style for a stronger and weaker lesson. Make notes on anything you would like to change, if applicable.

This task was inspired by Kate Protsenko's IATEFL Glasgow 2017 presentation. She put her feedback and that of her colleagues into WordItOut, a word cloud generator, to find out which words dominated. Read more in this summary of the presentation: sandymillin.wordpress.com/2017/04/17/iatefl-glasgow-2017-teacher-training/.

Observation: Written feedback 2: The clarity of comments

Task: 20 minutes
Reflection: 20 minutes

Read a range of written feedback, from different trainers if possible, or from different points in your own training career if not. Try to look at a minimum of three different documents.

- How clear do you think the comments are in the written feedback? How do you define a 'clear' comment? What has influenced your definition of clarity in comments?
- Are there differences between the documents? Are there differences within the same document? Why do you think this is?
- What do you think makes the comments more or less clear? For example, are there descriptions of specific incidents from the lessons? Are symbols used?
- Do you notice any patterns in which comments are particularly clear or less clear? For example, those connected to student interaction might be clear, but those to setting up activities might be less clear.
- Are there any specific comments which are particularly unclear? How could you make them clearer?
- If you are looking at feedback from other trainers, is there anything they do to make comments clear which you don't? Could you incorporate this into your own feedback?
- What do you think of the layout of the feedback form(s)? Do you think this has any influence on the kind and clarity of comments included? Would you change the form? Why (not)? If yes, how?
- Having read this feedback, is there anything you want to change about the clarity of comments in your own written feedback in future?

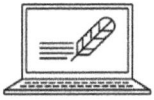

Write three tips you would give to a new trainer to help them make comments in written feedback as clear as possible. Share them using the #ELTplaybook hashtag.

Talk about your definition of a 'clear' comment and whether this has changed over time.

Take a photo of the feedback form you used, and note what influence you think it has on the kind and clarity of comments written on it. Mention any changes you would make to it. Don't forget to ask permission if you want to share it.

Describe the patterns of clarity you noticed in your own comments and whether there is anything you want to change. If so, make a 2- or 3-point action plan outlining how you will do this.

Observation: Written feedback 3: Action points

Task and reflection: 20 minutes altogether

Choose a teacher that you have given written feedback to, preferably on at least two occasions. Re-read the feedback you gave them in each case with a particular focus on the action points you selected. Answer the following questions.

- How many action points did you give them? Do you think this was a realistic number? Why (not)?
- Did you prioritise areas to work on? If yes, how did you do this? If no, how did you ensure that trainees were not overwhelmed?
- Why did you choose those particular action points? On re-reading the rest of the feedback you gave them, would you still choose the same action points? Why (not)?
- How did you phrase the action points? For example, did you use statements, questions, bullet points, etc? Do you think they were clear to the teacher? Why (not)?
- What written or spoken support did you give the teacher to help them work on these action points?
- If you observed the same teacher again later, did you comment on any of the same action points? Was there an improvement in any of the areas you had mentioned? Why (not)?
- If you were to do the same observation again, is there anything you would change about the action points? For example, the points you chose, the wording you used, or the support you gave. Why (not)?
- What advice would you give to other trainers about writing action points?

Write three pieces of advice for a new trainer writing action points for the first time.

Choose one of the action points you gave. Describe the written or spoken support you gave the teacher to help them work on this point.

With the teacher's permission, share a photo of the action points using the #ELTplaybook hashtag. Comment on what you would or would not change if you wrote them again and why.

Write about the differences between the first and second observation with the same teacher in terms of the action points given and why you think these differences came about. If there were no differences, comment on why this might be the case.

Observation: Written feedback 4: Including the students

Task: 5 minutes
Reflection: 20 minutes

Take one set of written feedback you have given to a teacher. Highlight each time you mentioned the students in any way.

- What methods did you use to reference the students in your written feedback? For example, did you use seating diagrams and students' names? Did you refer to the group as a whole?
- Why did you choose these methods? Are there any others you would like to experiment with in future?
- Can you categorise the mentions in any way? For example, were the comments positive/negative? Were students mentioned in relation to something the teacher did? Did you notice any patterns related to when you do or don't mention the students?
- Did you refer to students in the positive or action points you gave to the teacher? Why (not)?
- Was there anywhere in the feedback where it would have been better to add/remove a reference to the students? Is yes, why?
- What percentage of this piece of written feedback explicitly refers to the students? Do you think you refer to them enough? Did you mention any individual students? Why (not)?
- Ideally, what do you think the balance should be between teacher-focused and student-focused comments in your written feedback? Why?
- Having analysed your mentions of students in this feedback, is there anything you would change in your written feedback in the future? Why (not)?

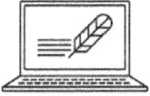

Using the #ELTplaybook hashtag, tell us when and why you might (not) want to refer to students in written feedback.

Describe the different ways that you referred to the students in your written feedback, and whether you noticed any patterns within your references.

Sketch a pie chart showing the percentage of this feedback which referred to students. Comment on what you think a good balance would be between teacher-focused and student-focused comments in written feedback and your reasons for thinking this.

Write about when you could have added or removed references to students in this piece of written feedback. Say why.

This task was inspired by Christian Tiplady's blog post 'Learner-centred observations of teachers', which you can read at sandymillin.wordpress.com/2018/10/14/learner-centred-observations-of-teachers-guest-post/.

Observation: Written feedback 5: What do you write about?

Task: 10 minutes
Reflection: 20 minutes

Re-read one set of written feedback you have given. Think about categories for the written comments you made, for example, using technology, teacher position, or examining language. Choose one colour for each category and highlight your feedback

- What categories did you choose? How many of them? Why these categories?
- Are there any categories you think should have been included but are missing from your comments?
- Did you notice anything surprising about the comments in each category?
- Within each category, can you see any patterns in the kind of comments you make or the wording you use? Is there anything you would like to change? Why (not)?
- How useful do you think your comments are in each category? Why? If there are comments that are not useful, why aren't they?
- Did the type of comments change as the observation progressed? Why (not)?

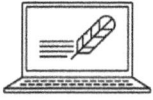

List example comments from one of the categories and say why these are (not) useful comments to make. Share your list using the #ELTplaybook hashtag.

Describe any patterns you noticed in the kind of comments you make and the wording you use.

With the permission of the teacher whose feedback it is, share a photo of part of the feedback. Comment on what you noticed about your comments in that section.

Write about what you would and wouldn't change about the kind of comments you make in one of the categories and why.

Observation: Spoken feedback 1: Balancing participation

Task and reflection: 30 minutes altogether

Think back to the last spoken feedback session you ran and answer the following questions.

- How did you invite trainee participation? When? Why?
- What kind of comments did trainees make? Do you consider them to have been superficial, deep or somewhere in between? Why?
- What questions did they ask? Why do you think they asked these questions? How useful do you think they were?
- What support did you provide for trainees to make comments or ask questions? What other support could you provide? For example, giving them prompts or question words to frame their thinking, or adding thinking time.
- What kind of comments did you make? What kind of questions did you ask? Looking back at the whole session, would you change any of them now?
- What was the balance of comments and questions? What do you think the balance should be?
- How do you think you came across? What kind of impression do you think your comments and questions made? Why? Is there anything you would like to change about this?
- Who do you think spoke the most: you or the trainee(s)? Are you happy with this balance? Why (not)?

Comment on how you (could) support trainees to be able to participate fruitfully in spoken feedback sessions. Share your ideas using the #ELTplaybook hashtag.

Talk about the kinds of questions you asked and comments you made during this spoken feedback session, and whether you would change any of them in hindsight.

Draw a set of scales to show the balance of who spoke during the feedback session. Note whether you were happy with this balance and why (not).

Write about how you think you came across in the spoken feedback session, why, and whether there is anything you would like to change about this.

Observation: Spoken feedback 2: The relationship with written feedback

Task: One spoken feedback session
Reflection: 30 minutes, plus the length of the recording

With the permission of the participants, record one of your spoken feedback sessions. Listen to the recording and look at the corresponding written feedback, if you gave any. Answer the following questions.

- Did you give both written and spoken feedback after this observation? Why (not)?
- Did you cover the same points in written and spoken feedback? Why (not)?
- Which areas did you spend the most time on in spoken feedback? Do these reflect the points you emphasised in written feedback? Why (not)?
- Was there anything you mentioned in written feedback which you think you should have discussed? Why didn't you?
- Was there anything you discussed in spoken feedback which you think you should also be in written feedback? Did you give written feedback that reflected this?
- Did anything surprise you when listening to the recording? What? Why?
- How similar or different do you think spoken and written feedback should be? Why?
- In general, when do you give spoken feedback? When do you give written feedback? Why?
- As a result of this reflection, is there anything you would like to change about your future spoken or written feedback processes? Why (not)?

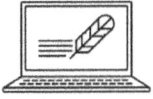

List three things you noticed that were similar or different between your written and spoken feedback. Say why you chose to highlight these areas.

Use the #ELTplaybook hashtag to tell us about whether you would like to make any changes to your spoken and written feedback as a result of this task.

Draw a flowchart of your spoken and written feedback processes, how they relate to each other, and why you give feedback in this way.

Write about whether you feel there was anything missing from your spoken or written feedback in this case, or whether you feel they reflected each other well. Say why.

Observation: Spoken feedback 3: What can go wrong?

Task: 20 minutes
Reflection: 25 minutes

For ten minutes, write a list of all of the things which could go wrong during spoken feedback, for example a trainee gets angry about your feedback, you run out of time to tell trainees the positive things about their lessons. For the next ten minutes, aim to write one solution for each possible problem.

- How easy was it for you to think of problems? And solutions? Why?
- Were there any problems you couldn't think of possible solutions for? Why do you think this was a challenge?
- Can you categorise the problems in any way? Are there any categories which have more problems in them than others? Why do you think this is?
- Have you experienced any of these problems? If yes, what did you do when they happened? How did you feel? How do you think the trainee(s) felt? Why? Would you change anything if you experienced the same problem again?
- Have you tried any of the solutions? How successful were they? Would you use them again? How did you feel? How do you think the trainee(s) felt? Why?
- Is there anything you would change about your spoken feedback process in the future as a result of thinking through what could go wrong? Why (not)? How useful did you find this process?

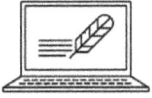

List three possible problems and the solutions you came up with.

Talk about what you learnt from the process of thinking through potential problems and possible solutions.

Draw one of the problems as a cartoon. Put the possible solution(s) around the cartoon and share it using the #ELTplaybook hashtag.

Describe a problem you have had during spoken feedback, how you resolved it at the time, and whether you would do anything differently if you faced the same problem again.

Observation: Spoken feedback 4: Input in feedback

Task: 5 minutes
Reflection: 20 minutes

After completing a spoken feedback session, make a note of the amount of time you spent reflecting on the lesson with the trainee(s), and what, if any, input you gave to help them with future lessons. Input might include giving them three specific tips to work on that action point, making an action plan together, or agreeing on somebody they could observe.

- Did you choose to include any input in your spoken feedback? If so, what? Why? How useful do you think it was for the trainee? If not, why not?
- How do you think the trainee felt about their spoken feedback in general? If you gave them input, do you think they were ready for it? Why (not)? How did they react to it? How likely do you think they are to use the input you gave?
- If you did include some input, had you planned it in advance or did you deliver it on the spot? What might the effect have been if you'd done the opposite?
- Did anything surprise you about the amount of time you spent on reflection compared to input in this case? If so, what?
- What do you think the balance between feedback and input should be? Do you normally include input in spoken feedback sessions or do you prefer to keep it separate? Why?
- What kind of input could you give during a spoken feedback session? For example, sharing a blog post link or demonstrating a technique. What could each type of input help trainees to understand?

Write about what you believe the ideal balance between feedback and input should be, and when and why you think input should be given.

Talk about three different ways of including input in a spoken feedback session and what they could help trainees to understand. Share your recording using the #ELTplaybook hashtag.

Draw a set of scales showing how you balanced input and feedback in this feedback session. Add notes about why you made that decision.

Describe the trainee's response to your spoken feedback in this case, including to any input you may have given. Say whether this would make you add or remove input in future spoken feedback sessions.

Observation: Spoken feedback 5: Varying feedback

Task: 10 minutes
Reflection: 20 minutes

List all the different ways you can think of to organise and run spoken feedback.
If you are short of ideas, Jo Gakonga has a list of ideas on her website:
www.elt-training.com/course?courseid=celta-trainer-resources.

- Which of the methods have you tried or have you seen other trainers use? What worked and didn't work when you used them?
- Which would you like to try? Do you have an upcoming feedback session where you could experiment with them?
- What is your favourite way of running spoken feedback? Why?
- What do you think are the advantages and disadvantages of each method?
- Can you categorise the methods you came up with? Are there any categories which are emptier or fuller? Why do you think this is?
- On a continuum from always delivering spoken feedback in the same way to trying something different every time, where do you think you lie? Why do you think this is? Would you like to move more towards one end or the other? Why (not)?

Compare two of the methods you have tried, stating what did and didn't work when you used them.

Describe your favourite way of organising and running spoken feedback and say why you like it.

Share a photo of your list using the #ELTplaybook hashtag. Note which of these ways you would like to try out in the future and why.

State how often you vary spoken feedback or if you don't vary it at all. Say why you think this is and whether you would like to change this or not.

Workshops and input sessions 1: Planning sessions

Task: 15 minutes
Reflection: 30 minutes

Think back to the last two training sessions you planned. Note down the steps you took to get from the initial fact of needing to put together a session to the final session which you then delivered.

- Were you happy with the session plans before you delivered them? What about afterwards? Why (not)?
- What form did your plan take for each of the two sessions (e.g. a lesson plan, a bulleted list, a set of PowerPoint slides)? In retrospect, how suitable was this form of plan?
- What information did you include in your plans (e.g. materials, timing, anticipated problems)? Is there anything that you could have included or left out?
- How efficient was your planning process in each case? Was it different at all for the two sessions? Why (not)?
- Were there any unnecessary steps to your planning? Was there anything which you ought to have done but didn't?
- What resources did you draw on when planning your sessions? How did you exploit them?
- Did you speak to anyone about your sessions before you delivered them? If yes, did they help you in any way? If no, do you think anybody could have helped you? Why (not)?
- How did your plans relate to the actual sessions as they happened? How would you explain any differences?
- How might you change your planning process for future sessions?

Describe the steps you went through to plan one of your sessions and whether you would change any of them in future.

Discuss the resources you used and/or the people that you spoke to in the process of planning one of your sessions and say how they influenced the final session.

Using the #ELTplaybook hashtag, share a photo or screenshot of one of your two plans with notes about the suitability of this type of plan to the type of session you were delivering.

Write about how you felt about your plan before one of the sessions, how the plan worked during the session, and how you felt about it afterwards, as well as how you might change your planning process in the future in light of what you have learnt.

Workshops and input sessions 2: Timing and pacing

Task: One session
Reflection: 30 minutes

During an input or feedback session, make a quick note of the time each activity takes. If it felt like the pace dragged for that activity, add a snail shell. If it felt rushed, add a lightning bolt. After the session, look back at your plan and annotations and answer the questions below.

- Did the activities take the amount of time you expected? Were any much longer or shorter? Why do you think that was?
- Did you manage to achieve your aims in the time available? Why (not)?
- If an activity felt slow, what caused this? Was it really necessary to slow down like this? Did it add to the session?
- If an activity felt rushed, why did this happen? Did the trainees lose out on anything because of the rush? Did it have a knock-on effect later in the session (or the training process if it covered a longer period of time)? If yes, how did you deal with it?
- If none of your activities have a snail shell or a lightning bolt next to them, what did you do at the planning stage or within the session to make sure that they were all timed and paced realistically?
- In retrospect, do you think your trainees would agree with your assessment of the pacing of the session?
- Were the timing and pacing of the session a result of planning or of circumstances within the session? Is there anything you should do differently to influence this in the future?
- Was there anything which surprised you when analysing your session in this way? Is it something you would consider doing again?

If your timing and pacing are generally realistic and beneficial to trainees, share three tips you have for other trainers about how to decide on this at the planning stage. If they are problematic for you, write three things you could try next time you plan a session to make your timing and pacing more realistic.

Talk about what you learnt from the process of analysing your timing and pacing in this way, as well as whether you would do it again.

Post an image of one of your snail shells or lightning bolts using the #ELTplaybook hashtag. Describe the related activity along with what effect the fact that it dragged or was rushed had on the trainees, either within the session or in the longer term.

Write about when and why the timing and pacing differed from what you anticipated before the session and what effect this had on whether you managed to achieve your aims within the time available.

Workshops and input sessions 3: Who's doing the work?

Task: 10 minutes
Reflection: 30 minutes

Look at the plan for some training you have recently done, either via a face-to-face session or online. Next to each stage of the training, make a note of the types of interaction that happened during the session, e.g. pair work, lecture, open-class work, forum discussion led by trainer.

- Why did you choose the particular types of interaction for each stage?
- What percentage of the session was conducted in each mode? How typical is this of your training? Was there anything surprising when you thought about the percentages, or does it match your expectations?
- What are the general benefits and drawbacks of each of the types of interaction you used when teacher training? How did they enhance or hinder your training in this particular case?
- How much variety did you include in the session? Do you think this was appropriate? Should you have varied it more or should you have reduced the amount of variety? Why?
- Are they any types of interaction which you could have included but didn't? What changes would that require if you ran the session again?
- How did your trainees respond to the different types of interaction? What impact do you think that had on their ability to learn from the training?
- Overall, who was doing the work in your session? What do you think of the balance between what you and the trainees did?

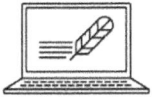

Choose one of the types of interaction you used in your session. Write about its benefits and drawbacks in a training context, and why you chose to use it in this session.

Talk about how varied your session was, whether you think this was appropriate, and whether you would change it in future.

Create a pie chart to show the percentage of your session you estimate was conducted in each mode. Make notes about what you noticed from drawing it. Share it using the #ELTplaybook hashtag.

Write about how you would or would not vary the interaction patterns if you ran the session again and how these patterns might influence the trainees' ability to learn from it.

Workshops and input sessions 4: Use of materials (or not!)

Task and reflection: 30 minutes altogether

Look back at a session you have previously done and answer the following questions. For the purposes of these questions, materials means anything used in the session that had to be created or copied, for example handouts, presentations or online tasks.

- What materials did you use? What did you use them for? Why?
- If you didn't use any materials, why did you choose this approach? What are the advantages and disadvantages of a materials-light or materials-free session?
- Which of the materials worked the way you planned in the session? Which didn't? Is there anything you would change in a future session?
- Were any of the materials you used unnecessary? Would your trainees have benefited from any extra materials?
- Could you have exploited any of the materials more? Could you have included what trainees brought to the session more?
- How accessible and useful were materials to the trainees? Consider language level, jargon, design, and any other criteria you can think of. Is there anything which it would be useful to change before running the session again?
- What principles do you follow when choosing or designing materials to use in your sessions?

List the principles you follow when choosing or designing materials for your sessions. Share them using the #ELTplaybook hashtag.

Talk about the potential advantages and disadvantages of a materials-light or materials-free session.

Upload some of the materials you used. Comment on how you used them in the session and whether it worked the way you planned.

Detail what you would keep the same and what you would change if you ran this session again, focusing on the way you used materials or your choice not to use materials.

Workshops and input sessions 5: Takeaways and follow-up

Task and reflection: 30 minutes altogether

Look at the plan for the next session you are going to run. Put yourself into the shoes of one of the people you think will be doing the training. Answer the following questions from their perspective.

- What have you learnt from the session? If you were telling a colleague about it, how would you summarise it?
- How will you remember this a few days after the session? Will you still remember it a few months later? Why (not)?
- If you received any materials, links, etc., do you think you will refer to them again? Why (not)?
- How relevant was the session to your current teaching context or one you will enter in the future? Why?
- What will you try out or think more about from the session? How easy will it be for you to do this? Will you need any extra help or support to do this? Will you need to be reminded to do it?
- How much information was in the session? Do you think it was the right amount? What would you add or remove? Why?
- Overall, did the session provide a good return on the time you invested in it?
- With your trainer hat on again, is there anything you would change in your session having considered these questions?
- Have you ever considered a session from a trainee's perspective before? Does this change how you think about it? Why (not)?

List ways that trainers can help trainees to retain and act upon the information from their sessions.

Describe what you plan to do to help trainees remember what you taught them in this specific session. Say why you think these strategies will help. If possible, check in with a trainee at some point after the session to find out whether the strategies you used worked.

Share a photo of your session plan using the #ELTplaybook hashtag. Comment on how it should link to the context of your trainees.

Write about your experience of the process of considering the session from the trainees' perspective and whether it changed anything about how you would run it.

Other aspects 1: Doing something different

Task and reflection: 20 minutes altogether

Look at the plan for the next training session/course you are going to do and choose some of the following questions to answer.

- Is there anything in the training room which you don't normally use but could? Or which you normally use but don't necessarily need to? Is it possible to arrange the room differently?

- Could you invite guests to join you for the training, either in person or via an online platform?

- Is it possible to incorporate more reading from methodology texts or clips from webinars or other related audio? Or less?

- How much of your own and trainees' experience do you explicitly include in your training? Could you exploit it more? Or less?

- Are there any new activities you have wanted to try out for a while? Is there a way to usefully incorporate them into your training?

- Can you use technology in a different way? Or not use it at all?

- How much do your trainees usually speak to others? Move around? Write notes? Can you change any of these things?

- What do your trainees usually take away from your sessions? Is there anything different they could take away this time?

- What effects do you think any of the changes you have come up with will have on the training? Which ones would you particularly like to try out? Are there any which you think wouldn't work? Why?

- How often do you do something different with your training? How do you feel about doing things differently? Why do you think this is?

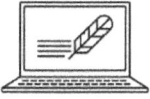

Write about the change which you are most likely to try out, as well as when and why.

Describe one of the differences you considered using but rejected. Say what it was and why you decided not to try it, as well as whether it could be used in a different context to the one you were thinking of originally.

Draw a mind-map of all of the possible tweaks you came up with for your training. Highlight the ones you would particularly like to try out.

Comment on your feelings about trying something different in your training, and why you think you feel this way.

Other aspects 2: Observation of other teachers

Task: 5 minutes
Reflection: 25 minutes

List all of the ways that you include observations of real classrooms in your training. This could be anything from a 2-minute video clip to a 2-hour live lesson, and the list could also say 'none'!

- When is observation included in your training? Why? If you don't include observation, why not?
- Is there anywhere you could add more observation? Is there anywhere you include it where it doesn't necessarily add anything to the training?
- Is it live or video-based? What are the advantages and disadvantages of each?
- Who are the trainees observing? Why are these people chosen for them to watch?
- How long are the observations? Why are they this length? Could trainees benefit from longer or shorter observations?
- In general, what are the benefits for trainees of observing other teachers? What are the drawbacks? If you include observations in your own training, what do you think your trainees specifically have gained from them?
- Do you give any particular tasks for observers to complete while they are observing? Why (not)? If you do, what tasks do you use and why?
- What opportunities did trainees have to discuss the observation before or afterwards? Was this enough? Why (not)?

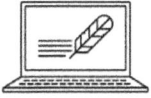

List two benefits and two drawbacks of including observation in training.

Using the #ELTplaybook hashtag, share your thoughts on the advantages and disadvantages of either live or video-based observation.

Take a photo of a possible task that trainees could do while observing other teachers. Say why it should be useful for them.

Write about the people who your trainees observe and why you chose those people for them to watch. Alternatively, write about why you don't include observation in your training sessions.

Other aspects 3: Dealing with challenges

Task and reflection: 30 minutes altogether

Think back over your career as a teacher trainer so far. Choose one incident which was particularly challenging for you. Write a description of what happened. Try to be as objective as possible. Use the questions below to help you.

- Who was involved (e.g. you, a trainee, a student, a manager)? How did those people (seem to) feel at the time? What contributed to this?
- Were there any witnesses to the situation? What did they do? Was it appropriate for them to see what was happening? Why (not)?
- Where did it take place? Who controlled the choice of location? Did the location have any influence on the situation?
- When did it happen? Had anything in particular happened before? Was anything expected to happen afterwards? Did any of that influence the situation?
- Step by step, what happened?
- How did you react at each stage of the situation? Do you think this was appropriate? Why (not)?
- Did you move towards a resolution? Why (not)? If yes, how? If not, how did it end?
- In hindsight, is there anything you would do differently? Why (not)?
- What did you learn from the situation?
- What advice would you give other trainers if they found themselves in a similar situation?

Describe how challenging situations can be influenced by the place and time that they happen and by who is present at the time.

Talk about what you believe a trainer should do if they find themselves in a similar challenging situation. If you choose to share details of a particular situation, don't forget to ask permission.

Draw a picture that summarises the situation for you and share it using the #ELTplaybook hashtag. Write notes about why you chose to draw this particular picture and what it represents.

Write about what you would do if you found yourself in this situation again, and why.

Other aspects 4: Trainer health and wellbeing

Task: 10 minutes
Reflection: 20 minutes

List the things you (would like to) do to look after your physical and mental health and wellbeing when doing training. For example, taking regular exercise breaks, or maintaining distance by only giving work contact details to trainees, not personal ones.

- How do the things you have listed help you maintain your own health and wellbeing?
- Which of them are more relevant to short-term training (e.g. a few hours)? Which to long-term training (e.g. a course that runs over many months)? Which are relevant to both?
- Which of them do you do regularly? How do you incorporate them into your schedule?
- Has your attitude to your health and wellbeing changed over the time that you have been training? Why (not)?
- Which would you like to do more? What steps can you take to add them to your life?
- What impact do you think seeing a trainer who does or doesn't look after their own health and wellbeing could have on trainees? Why?
- What advice would you give to a new trainer about maintaining their health and wellbeing?

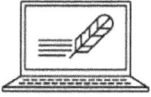

Write one piece of advice you would give to a new trainer about maintaining their health and wellbeing. Say whether it is more appropriate to short- or long-term training and why. Share it using the #ELTplaybook hashtag.

Talk about three of the things on your list. Say how they help you to ensure your own wellbeing.

Draw a trainer who does or doesn't look after their health and wellbeing. Add notes to say what impact working with this trainer might have on trainees.

Make a health and wellbeing action plan for the next training you will do. Include two things you will continue doing and two things you would like to start doing.

Other aspects 5: Beyond the training room

Task: 10 minutes
Reflection: 30 minutes

Draw a diagram showing the connections between your training room and the outside world, based on one particular session. This could be things coming into the training room (for example, methodology books, research, or trainee experience) or leaving it (for example, the particular ideas you would like to trainees to take away from your session, the things you would like them to produce during the session or specific feelings and impressions they might have after the session).

- What do you think of the range of things coming into and going out of your training room? Is there anything you would like to add or which you think should be removed? Why?
- Thinking about what comes into the training room, how do you exploit these things? Why do you choose to use them?
- Do the books and other resources brought into the training room represent trainees' contexts accurately? Areas to consider might include gender, race or sexual identities. Why (not)?
- If they are representative, is this something you have consciously worked on? If not, would you change it in future? How?
- What impact do you think (lack of) representation in training materials might have on your trainees?
- What are the connections between what is coming in and what is going out of the room? Who makes these connections (i.e. the trainer or the trainees)? When? How? Why?
- How do you think the diagram you drew will change/has changed over time as your experience as a trainer increases/has increased?

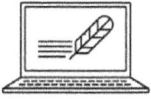

For one of the things coming into the training room, describe why you use it and how you exploit it.

Talk about the connections between what comes into and goes out of your training room, who makes these connections, and how.

Using the #ELTplaybook hashtag, share the diagram you drew. Comment on whether it was a useful process to draw it and why (not).

Write about whether you think representation of trainees' contexts in the material that comes into the training room is important for your trainees and why (not).

Appendix 1: Acknowledging sources

In the age of the internet and easy sharing, it can be easy to forget to acknowledge your sources, but it's important to make it a habit to do this, as well as demonstrating it to your students and trainees too.

The examples of citations below are the formats you will probably find most useful while using this book. They are loosely based on APA (American Psychological Association) citations. You can find full information on APA at www.bibme.org/apa.

For materials or images taken from books
In line with text:
(Author's last name, year of publication: page number)
For example: (Harmer, 2007: 248)

In a list of references, organised alphabetically by surname:
Author's last name, Author first name (year of publication) *Title of source*. Publisher
For example:
Harmer, Jeremy (2007) *The Practice of English Language Teaching* 4th edition. Pearson Longman

For material from the internet
Check the website for permissions, as sometimes you may not be allowed to reuse an image or text.

In line with text:
If known: (Author's last name, date of publication)
For example: (Blanchard, 2017)
If unknown: (name of the website, accessed [date])
For example: (www.bibme.org, accessed 22nd August 2017)

In a list of references, organised alphabetically by surname:
Note: Check that you are linking to the original page, not just a link from the search page.
Author's last name, Author first name if known/Author unknown (date of publication if known/Date unknown) 'Title of source'. Retrieved from URL. Accessed on [the date you found it]
You can often see the date of publication within the URL, as in the example below.

For example:

Author unknown (Date unknown) 'Your Ultimate APA Format Guide & Generator' Retrieved from www.bibme.org/apa. Accessed on 22nd August 2017

Blanchard, Amy (2017, May 21) 'Boardwork (guest post)' Retrieved from sandymillin.wordpress.com/2017/05/21/boardwork-guest-post/. Accessed on 22nd August 2017

Images:

One of the most popular ways for owners to give permission to reuse their work is called Creative Commons. They have different types of licence, with symbols to help you understand them. All of the information is available on their website (www.creativecommons.org/share-your-work/licensing-types-examples/, accessed 22nd August 2017). Many images on Flickr are shared this way. This includes those from ELTpics at www.flickr.com/photos/eltpics, which is designed for teachers to reuse. Here is one of my own photos from the collection:

Photo taken from www.flickr.com/eltpics by Sandy Millin, used under a CC Attribution Non-Commercial license

(Note: As *ELT Playbook Teacher Training* is being sold, it doesn't comply with the conditions of the CC non-commercial license, but as it is my own photo, I do not need to get permission.)

If you include your own images in something you are sharing, it's worth stating this too. For example: 'Image from my personal collection.'

Appendix 2: Getting permission

Some of the tasks in the book ask you to take photos or record videos. If you do this, it's important to get permission from anybody whose face appears in the images before you share them (or from anybody whose work you use). It's also good practice to ask for permission if you would like to share photos or videos of premises that you do not own, as what is shown in the image or recording could reflect back on the owners. The permission slips below are examples you could use to let people know how you will use photos or videos. Feel free to translate them or adapt them to suit your context.

For photos or videos of under-18s
I am planning to take photos of your child for my professional development as a teacher. I would like to share it on my blog, available at sandymillin.wordpress.com, so other teachers can give me feedback. Please circle the statement you agree with.

I give/do not give my permission for you to take photos of my child.
I give/do not give my permission for you to share photos of my child on your blog.

For photos or videos of adults
I would like to video our feedback session for my professional development as a trainer. Afterwards, if I have your permission, I plan to share it on my blog, available at sandymillin.wordpress.com, so other trainers can give me feedback. Please circle the statement you agree with.

I give/do not give my permission for you to video our session.
I give/do not give my permission for you to share the video on your blog.

For the owners of premises you would like to film in
To help my development as a trainer, I would like to take photos of my classroom and write about it on my blog, available at sandymillin.wordpress.com, so other teachers can give me feedback. Please circle the statement you agree with.

I give/do not give my permission for you to take photographs in our school.
I give/do not give my permission for you to share the photographs on your blog.

Appendix 3: Further reading

The following books may be particularly useful to readers of *ELT Playbook Teacher Training*:

- Magnus Coney (2018) *The Lazy Teacher Trainer's Handbook*. the round (e-book)
- Roger Gower, Diane Phillips and Steve Walters (2005) *Teaching Practice: A Handbook for Teachers in Training*. Macmillan ELT – particularly Chapter 9 'For the new trainer'
- John Hughes (2015) *A Practical Introduction to Teacher Training in ELT*. Pavilion Publishing and Media
- Steve Mann and Steve Walsh (2016) *Reflective Practice in English Language Teaching: Research-Based Principles and Practices*. Routledge
- Martin Parrott (1993) *Tasks for Language Teachers: A Resource Book for Training and Development*. Cambridge University Press
- Mick Randall with Barbara Thornton (2001) *Advising and Supporting Teachers*. Cambridge University Press
- Craig Thaine (2010) *Teacher Training Essentials: Workshops for Professional Development*. Cambridge University Press
- Michael J Wallace (1991) *Training Foreign Language Teachers: A Reflective Approach*. Cambridge University Press
- Tony Wright and Rod Bolitho (2008) *Trainer Development*. lulu.com

You can also find useful resources on these websites:

- ttedsig.iatefl.org/ - The IATEFL Teacher Training and Education Special Interest Group has a series of webinars. The most recent information about the webinars is available via their Twitter account @IATEFL_TTEdSIG.
- www.elt-training.com - Choose the 'for trainers' category for a range of resources from Jo Gakonga.
- www.teacherfeedback.org - Another website created by Jo Gakonga for teacher trainers, focussed specifically on the feedback process.
- akoaotearoa.ac.nz/ako-aotearoa/ako-aotearoa/resources/pages/esol-teaching-skills-taskbook-unit - Craig Thaine's *ESOL Teaching Skills Taskbook* has a series of tasks which you could use in workshops and input sessions.

If you do not have any written feedback to analyse, you can find a range of lesson recordings at 'Lessons you can watch online' on my blog: sandymillin.wordpress.com/2017/11/11/lessons-you-can-watch-online/

If you are working with relatively inexperienced teachers, the tasks in *ELT Playbook 1* and the further reading list in Appendix 4 of that book may also be useful when designing sessions and considering how to give feedback. See eltplaybook.wordpress.com

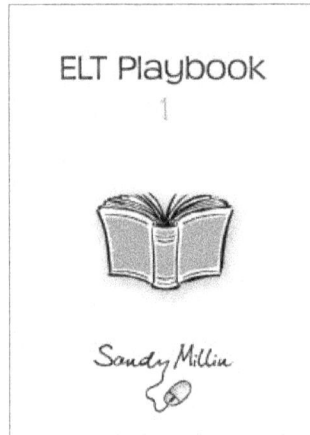

ELT Playbook
1

Sandy Millin

Appendix 4: Recording your progress

I hope that you will find *ELT Playbook Teacher Training* useful, but I know that that is not always enough for potential employers. To that end, I have created a series of badges which you can claim as evidence that you have completed each set of tasks, and subsequently the whole book. They can be displayed on your CV or social media profiles. Here are previews of the badges for this book:

To get your personalised badge for any one section:

- Complete all five tasks in a single section, for example 'What is training?'
- Share your reflections on each task in whatever form(s) you choose and on whichever platform, for example as blogposts and videos shared via Twitter. Don't forget to include the #ELTplaybook hashtag on Twitter or Instagram, or to share it on the ELT Playbook group if you're on facebook.
- Tweet, Facebook or Instagram links to all five reflections in a single post on your social media of choice. Start with the phrase 'Badge please!' and include your full name as you'd like it to appear on the badge.
- I'll send you a personalised badge including your name and the date of issue.
- If you haven't heard from me for a couple of weeks, please tag me again, as I'm a one-man-band and may miss your post! I'll try to keep up as well as I can.

To get your personalised badge for the whole book:

- Tweet, Facebook or Instagram links to all six badges with your name on in a single post on your social media of choice, or write a comment on this blogpost. Start with the phrase 'Badge please!' and include your full name as you'd like it to appear on the badge.
- As above, I'll send you a personalised badge including your name and the date of issue.
- If you haven't heard from me for a couple of weeks, please tag me again, as I'm a one-man-band and may miss your post! I'll try to keep up as well as I can.

Good luck!

www.ingramcontent.com/pod-product-compliance
Lightning Source LLC
Chambersburg PA
CBHW022016080426
42733CB00007B/623